The Big Little Devotional Guide

BEAUTIFUL WORLD

Little
WORSHIP
Company

Contents

Little WORSHIP Company

Discovering GOD together

At **Little Worship Company**, our heart is to inspire and delight children with a knowledge of God, and to support them as they begin to take their first steps of faith. We also want to help parents as they walk with their children on this wonderful journey. Our range of beautifully-crafted, Biblically-based resources have been designed with the whole family in mind, so that all God's children, little ones and bigger ones, can discover more of God and His incredible love together.

There are four stunning DVDs that make up **Little Worship Company** Series 1:

- **Amazing Me** • **Beautiful World**
- Praise Party • **Wonderful Day**

This devotional guide has been written for use alongside the **Little Worship Company: Beautiful World** DVD. In this book, you and your family are invited to journey with our hosts, Hal and Mr. and Mrs. Looyah, as they explore the wonderful world God made together.

Welcome to Beautiful World!

Our world is amazing! **Little Worship Company: Beautiful World** Devotional Guide leads you and your family through the Bible's creation story, inspiring wonder in the incredible world we live in and helping us to see the God who made, knows and loves it – and who made, knows and loves us too.

How to use this resource

To make the most of this resource, choose a time of the day or week which suits you and your family. It might be just before bed, just after lunch or sometime over the weekend.

- **Watch a chapter from the DVD.** Each chapter will include a short slot from Hal and a worship song.

- **Read through the accompanying Bible verse** and short, family-friendly reflection, found in this devotional guide.

- **As a family, talk through the discussion question together.** Close with the short prayer found at the bottom of the page.

Each reflection includes a simple craft or recipe suggestion to go with it. You could do this as part of the reflection, or at another time to remind you of some of the ideas you've been exploring.

What else is in this resource?

As well as all-age devotions, you'll find a little 'big' thought that draws on the same themes but is aimed specifically at adults. Each one includes suggestions for further reflection and a short prayer. This could be something you reflect on while your child engages in the craft, or you might choose to read it over a cup of tea, by yourself, later on.

At **Little Worship Company**, we want to provide you with practical ideas for making your faith part of family life. In this book, you'll find some of our best tips for enjoying God's wonderful world **(page 23)** and ideas for looking after God's amazing creation **(page 37)**.

Old or young, big or small –
every single one of us is precious to God!

You'll probably spot a few LOVE BUGS on our pages. They might be little – but they remind us of God's BIG love for us.

Beautiful World

Genesis 1:3 (MSG)

God spoke: "Light!" And light appeared.

Wow, Mum! The sky's turning red!

That's the sunset, Hal. I think it's God's way of showing us how beautiful and special the light is.

Do you have a light switch in your house? Or a night light by your bed? What happens when you switch it on? The room is filled with light! There are lots of things which give us light. Sunshine. Torches. Twinkly Christmas lights. We don't always think about light. But we notice when it's not there.

The Bible says that God made the world and the first thing He made was light. Light is really important to us. It helps us to see things – like all the amazing colours in the world. And that's not all. Trees and flowers need light to grow – and so do we! The sun's light keeps us healthy, happy and warm. Light is part of God's beautiful world. **Isn't God amazing?**

TALK TOGETHER

How many things can you think of that give light? How does light make you feel? Thank God for light every time you flick a light switch!

MAKE TOGETHER

God made light and colour. Get a piece of paper and make your own light picture. Drip poster paint on your picture (you may need to water it down) and blow it in different directions with a straw to make stars. If you mix in a small amount of PVA glue to the paint, then you can add glitter to make it sparkly too.

LITTLE

PRAY TOGETHER

WOW, GOD! Thank you for giving us light. Thank you for painting the world in different colours. Thank you that I can see and enjoy Your beautiful world. **Amen.**

Beautiful World

TIME TO REFLECT

Genesis 1:1-5 *(read more in John 1:1-5, 9)*

In the beginning God created the heavens and the earth. Now the earth was formless and empty, darkness was over the surface of the deep, and the Spirit of God was hovering over the waters.

And God said, 'Let there be light,' and there was light. God saw that the light was good, and He separated the light from the darkness. God called the light 'day', and the darkness He called 'night'. And there was evening, and there was morning – the first day.

Genesis opens in darkness and nothingness. God is there, His Spirit hovering over the waters. And then He speaks those first, famous words: *"let there be light"*. Suddenly, the darkness is driven away and the stage is set for creation to follow.

It's impossible to overstate the importance of light to our world. It helps us see. It provides warmth and security.

FUNDAMENTALLY, LIGHT BRINGS LIFE.

Plants, which play such a critical role in our ecosystem, need light to grow and thrive. And we, too, need the sun's light in our bones and bodies to grow and thrive. Put simply – without light, we can't live.

The God of light, then, is the God of life. He is its source and sustainer. But it's clear from Scripture that the life God gives is more than just mechanical. As humans, we're born with an inbuilt sense that there's more to life than simply breathing, eating and sleeping. But what that 'something' is – that's been the source of endless debate, almost since time began. The Bible makes it clear that the answer is found in God. Throughout Scripture, God is associated with light – supremely in Jesus, the *"light of the world"* (John 8:12). His light shows us what's true – of God, of ourselves, of what the world is and of what it could be. It shows us which way we should go. And it overcomes the darkness – in ourselves, as well as in the world around us. In the beginning, God kick-started creation with His light. And as we live by the light of our marvellous Creator, so we can truly find life – and live it to the full.

TIME TO ACT

1   Write down the word 'light'. Spend a few minutes noting down everything that light makes you think of – whether that's what light does, or how it makes you feel.

Think about how Jesus called Himself the *"light of the world"* (John 8:12). How do your ideas about light help you to understand Jesus – who He is and what He does? Use these ideas to praise and thank Him.

2   In Matthew 5:14, Jesus called *us* the light of the world. Look back over your list of 'light' ideas. How does it help you to understand what we are called to as Jesus' followers in the world?

TIME TO PRAY

God of light,
I praise You because You are everything I need.

Thank you that You are as constant as the sunrise, giving me light and life each new morning.

Amen.

ONLY GOT A MINUTE?

- When God says, *"let there be light,"* the darkness is driven away.

- Without light, we can't live.

- The God of light is the God of life, the source and sustainer of all things.

- Jesus is called the *"light of the world"* but He also called *us* to be the light of the world. What might that mean?

Jeremiah 31:35 (LWC)

God makes the biggest and best waves – listen to them roar!

Wow! Look at the ocean! It goes on forever!

Yep – it's big alright! But our God who made it is even BIGGER!

What's the biggest thing you've ever seen in your life? A house? A block of flats? A skyscraper? These are pretty big. But there are some amazing things in our world which are even bigger!

Think of mountains. They tower so high that they get lost in the clouds. In fact, the world's biggest mountain, Everest, is as tall as twenty skyscrapers stacked on top of each other! But that's nothing compared to the oceans. The Pacific Ocean is wider than *all* the countries of the world put together – and it goes so deep that if Mount Everest sat on the ocean floor, it still wouldn't reach the surface! But the Bible says that, as big as they are, God is even *bigger*. He made the mountains and the oceans. And He holds them *all* in His hands. **Isn't God amazing?**

TALK TOGETHER

Look at a map of the world or a globe together. Get a sense of how big the world is and the size of the oceans. Look up pictures of mountain ranges online. As you look at our huge world, remember that God is even bigger!

MAKE TOGETHER

God made the huge mountains and oceans. Make a mountain range collage. Cut up lots of triangles in different sizes and different shades of grey/black/brown. Stick them onto a piece of A4 paper so that they are overlapping to look like a mountain range. Colour the tops with white chalk to look like snow. Thank God for His amazing creations!

Why not ask a grown-up to write a Bible verse for you?
In one hand God holds deep caves... in the other hand he grasps the high mountains. *Psalm 95:4 (MSG)*

PRAY TOGETHER

WOW, GOD! Thank you for big mountains and enormous oceans! Thank you that You are bigger than all of them, and that You hold them – and me – in Your hands. **Amen.**

LITTLE

Beautiful World

TIME TO REFLECT

Genesis 1:6-10 (*read more in Mark 4:35-41*)

*And God said, 'Let there be a vault between the waters to separate water from water.'
So God made the vault and separated the water under the vault from the water above it.
And it was so. God called the vault 'sky'. And there was evening, and there was morning –
the second day.*

*And God said, 'Let the water under the sky be gathered to one place, and let dry ground appear.'
And it was so. God called the dry ground 'land', and the gathered waters he called 'seas'.
And God saw that it was good.*

For most of us, our experience of the sea is probably at the water's edge, enjoying gentle waves lapping on the shore. However, if you've been out on the ocean – especially in windy conditions – you'll appreciate something of its might. Throughout Scripture, the seas are seen as evidence of God's awesomeness. It's not just the size and scale of the oceans – although that would be enough. It's the oceans' power, their enormous waves truly terrifying to behold. In Biblical times, the seas inspired a healthy fear, and the God of creation even more so. His voice raised up the waves, and with a word He stilled them too. The seas were mighty – and their God was even mightier.

THE GOD OF THE OCEANS IS UNDOUBTEDLY POWERFUL. BUT SCRIPTURE REMINDS US THAT HE IS LOVING TOO.

There are several miracles in the Bible which involve God commanding the waters – for example, Moses and the Israelites crossing the Red Sea as they flee Egypt, or Joshua leading the people through the Jordan and into the Promised Land. In the gospels, Jesus and His friends are out on the Sea of Galilee when a sudden storm whips up the waves, leaving the disciples fearing for their lives. But a word from Jesus calms the storm – and the disciples' fearful hearts. This is something we must remember. The God we worship is almighty. Powerful. Strong. But that doesn't make Him aloof, or angry, or unfeeling. His might is tempered by His love, His power by His wonderful promises to us. The God of creation holds the oceans in His hands. But that's not all He holds – He holds us too.

TIME TO ACT

1   Psalm 46:10 says:

Be still and know that I am God.

Fill a bowl with water. Stir it around to make waves and then watch as it calms. As you do so, think about how God is mightier than the oceans. Invite His Spirit to give you His peace in whatever you might be experiencing.

2   Jesus said that our faith could move mountains (Matthew 17:20). It is not the strength of our faith as much as the size of our God that makes the difference. Talk to God about the challenges facing you, your church family and your nation. Is God asking you to take a step of faith in the midst of these?

TIME TO PRAY

God of the oceans,
I praise You for Your incredible power and for Your indescribable love.

Thank you that I have nothing to fear while You are beside me.

Amen.

ONLY GOT A MINUTE?

- God created the untameable oceans.

- His voice raised up the waves, and with a word He stilled them too.

- The seas are mighty, but our God is even mightier.

- The God of creation holds the oceans in His hands.

- God holds us in His hands too.

BIG

Beautiful World

Isaiah 55:12 (LWC)

The **mountains** and the **hills** will shout **loud songs** – and the **trees** **clap** their hands.

Wow! The trees are covered in flowers! They're amazing!

Yes, Hal. They are beautiful. And God made them all!

Have you ever seen juicy strawberries growing on a plant? Or shiny apples on a tree? Have you ever seen daisies and buttercups growing in the grass? If you have, then you'll know that all kinds of wonderful things grow out of the soil. And they were all made by God!

The Bible says that God filled the world with all kinds of growing things, from big, tall trees to bright, colourful flowers. They're not just beautiful to see and smell. They provide us with everything we need to live well – like food, shelter and even clean air. And not just us, but millions of animals, birds and insects too! Trees and plants are part of God's beautiful world. **Isn't God amazing?**

TALK
TOGETHER

Go out into your garden or to the nearest park. Talk about the different things you can see growing there – trees, flowers, vegetables or grass. Or go to the fresh fruit and vegetable section of your supermarket. How many different types can you find? Say thank you to God for all the things you discover!

MAKE
TOGETHER

God made all kinds of amazing trees and flowers! Make your own 3D daffodils. Cut out cardboard petals and use small yoghurt pots for the trumpets and lolly sticks for the stems.

PRAY
TOGETHER

WOW, GOD! Thank you for tall trees and beautiful flowers. Thank you for juicy fruit and tasty vegetables. Thank you that You give us everything that we will ever need. **Amen.**

Beautiful World

TIME TO REFLECT

Genesis 1:11-13; 29-30

Then God said, 'Let the land produce vegetation: seed-bearing plants and trees on the land that bear fruit with seed in it, according to their various kinds.' And it was so. The land produced vegetation: plants bearing seed according to their kinds and trees bearing fruit with seed in it according to their kinds. And God saw that it was good. And there was evening, and there was morning – the third day.

Then God said, 'I give you every seed-bearing plant on the face of the whole earth and every tree that has fruit with seed in it. They will be yours for food. And to all the beasts of the earth and all the birds in the sky and all the creatures that move along the ground – everything that has the breath of life in it – I give every green plant for food.' And it was so.

The created world teaches us about the Creator. And the millions of wonderful things that spring from the soil speak volumes. God is a designer *par excellence*. The shapes, the sizes, the colours, the scents... they all reflect a designer with a flair for the spectacular. Not to mention the wonderful tastes. Any walk through a garden in bloom is a multisensory delight. But He's more than an artist. In this account of God's third day of creation, there's a small phrase which marks God out as a flawless engineer. It's not just that He made plants and trees. He made them 'seed-bearing'. In other words, as God created them, He put in them the ability to reproduce year on year, and in abundance.

This act of creation, so thoughtfully engineered, shows us a generous God. He loves to give – and give plentifully. But it also suggests something else. On the third day, God creates trees and plants. And then, on the sixth day, He gives them to the newly-created people, animals and birds so that they will have all they need to live. This goes beyond generosity. The traditional term for this is 'benevolence'. It literally means 'willing us good'. The trees and plants show a God who's been thinking of us since before we were even created and who is committed to our provision and care. We might wonder what God is like – whether He's really as good as the Bible makes out. But creation shows us it's true.

EVERY FRUIT-BEARING TREE AND SEED-BEARING PLANT LEAVES US IN NO DOUBT THAT THE GOD OF GROWING THINGS IS ROOTING FOR US.

TIME TO ACT

1 As you walk around your community, be mindful of the trees and plants you see. As you look at them, thank God for His beautiful creation and in His extraordinary care.

2 Good things grow in all seasons – even if we can't see them. Likewise, it's not always obvious to see what God is doing during our own 'winter' months – but we know that we can trust in His faithfulness and in His ability to work all things together for good.

Take some time to look back at the ways God has provided for and led you in the past – in the tough times as well as the good. Thank God for His care. Can these reflections encourage you in the present?

TIME TO PRAY

God of growing things,
I praise You for Your generosity and kindness.

Thank you that You give us everything that we need, in every season of our lives.

Amen.

ONLY GOT A MINUTE?

- The world around us teaches us that our God is generous.

- The beauty of creation shows us God's creativity.

- Seed-bearing plants and trees demonstrate God's commitment to our provision and care.

- Good things grow in all seasons – even if we can't see them.

- The God of all growing things is rooting for us.

What a
**wildly
wonderful
world,**
God!
You made
it all.

Psalm 104:24
(The Message)

What a wonderful world

ENJOYING GOD'S CREATION AS A FAMILY

Nothing beats going out and enjoying God's beautiful world!

Why not try a few of these with your family?

- **Go on a 'wonder walk'.** Go to the woods, the countryside or the seaside. Or simply walk about your own community. Be intentional about spotting the nature all around you. Why not turn it into a treasure hunt? Find something beginning with each letter of the alphabet, or in each colour of the rainbow.

- **Make the most of each season.** Walk through bluebell woods in spring. Pick blackberries in late summer – they grow everywhere, even in cities! Collect conkers in autumn. Make a snowman in winter.

- **Get growing.** Plant bulbs in pots or in the garden together and watch the flowers grow. Grow fruit and vegetables from seed. Start them off in pots on the windowsill, then plant them out as they get bigger. And then enjoy picking and eating them when the time comes!

- **Meet the animals.** Visit a farm, zoo, aquarium or even just a pet shop. Talk about what you like about the animals, birds or fish that you see there. Thank God for making them.

- **Dig a little deeper...** Dig up the soil in the garden to spot creepy crawlies. Go rock pooling at the seaside to search for tiny crabs and sea creatures. Look (from a safe distance!) into rivers – can you spot any fish swimming there?

- **Find out more!** There are so many wonderful nature programmes available on TV or online. Watch them together. Talk about what you see and thank God for His amazing creations! Go to the library and flick through nature books. What fun facts can you find out?

- **Go stargazing.** This is easiest in the winter when it gets dark earlier. On a clear night, get out sleeping bags and make warm drinks. Put on coats, hats and scarves. Lie down in the garden and look at all the different stars you can see.

- **Make nature art.** When you go out, pick up fallen leaves, feathers, sticks, seeds, petals... whatever you can find! Take them home and turn them into a nature collage. Make seaside art at the beach. Collect shells and seaweed and use them to make a picture in the sand.

Psalm 147:4-5 (LWC)

He knows how many stars there are. He gives names to all of them. God is great!

I can see a star! And another one! And another one!

Yes, Hal. There are more stars out there than we can count. But God knows how many there are. He made them!

Our world can feel like a pretty big place. But it's teeny tiny compared to space! We live on planet Earth. Our planet is just one, small part of a big, amazing universe. Look into the night sky and you can see other planets, moons and thousands of bright, shining stars.

Human beings have been studying space for a long, LONG time. However hard we try, we'll never know all there is to know about our universe. We don't even know how many stars there are – it's impossible to count them all! But God knows. He's the one that made them. The Bible says that He put the stars in the sky, one by one, and that He calls them by name. And He knows *your* name too! **Isn't God amazing?**

TALK TOGETHER

If it's a clear night, look up into the sky. Can you see the stars? Are any brighter than the rest? Think about how God knows how many stars are in the sky – and how He knows you too!

MAKE TOGETHER

God sees and knows the whole universe. Cut out cardboard stars and either make them out of different colours or cover them with silver foil. Hang them at different lengths on a coat hanger to make a mobile/decoration for your room.

LITTLE

PRAY TOGETHER

WOW, GOD! Thank you for the bright sun.
Thank you for the twinkling stars. Thank you that You know every bit of our universe – and that You know me too. **Amen.**

Beautiful World

TIME TO REFLECT

Genesis 1:14-19 *(read more in Psalm 8)*

And God said, "Let there be lights in the vault of the sky to separate the day from the night, and let them serve as signs to mark sacred times, and days and years, and let them be lights in the vault of the sky to give light on the earth." And it was so. God made two great lights – the greater light to govern the day and the lesser light to govern the night. He also made the stars. God set them in the vault of the sky to give light on the earth, to govern the day and the night, and to separate light from darkness. And God saw that it was good. And there was evening, and there was morning – the fourth day.

Humankind has long been fascinated by the Universe. For millennia, people have been gazing up into the night sky, studying the stars to seek answers to their big questions. In the last hundred years of human history this fascination has only increased, with moon landings and space probes opening up exciting possibilities for understanding life beyond planet Earth. And yet the Universe remains a mystery – the distant constellations a reminder of how much more there is to know and explore. Perhaps that's why it provides such inspiration in Scripture as a way of comprehending God's greatness.

THE UNIVERSE IS THE BIGGEST THING WE SEE – THE THING FURTHEST FROM OUR GRASP, INTELLECTUALLY AND PHYSICALLY. BUT GOD CREATED IT.

He put the stars in their place and He calls them by name. There is nothing God cannot do, and nothing He does not know.

But it's clear from Scripture that there's a bigger mystery out there than even the Universe – and that's God's love for us. *"When I consider your heavens, the work of your fingers,"* the psalmist writes, *"what is mankind that you are mindful of them?"* (from Psalm 8:3-4). The Hebrew word for 'mindful' speaks of God's attention and loving kindness. He sees us. He knows us. And there's more. The King James Version translates Psalm 8:4 as *"what is the son of man, that Thou visitest him?"* It's a word that reminds us how this great and awesome God put aside His splendour to become human like us. The God who knows the limits of the Universe knows our limits too. He understands our every thought and weakness. And this majestic God who brought about the entire Universe is still with us now.

TIME TO ACT

1　There's nothing like gazing into the night sky to make us aware of our own smallness and seeming insignificance. And yet we are precious to God. Take some time to praise God for His awesome love for us.

2　Cut out some star shapes to use in your prayers. Write on them the names of people you want to pray for and place them around the house. Remember that God knows them – that He knows their needs and He cares for them.

TIME TO PRAY

God of the Universe,
I praise You for Your greatness and majesty.

Thank you that nothing in all creation is hidden from Your knowledge or Your wonderful love.

Amen.

BIG

ONLY GOT A MINUTE?

- The Universe is the biggest thing we see. It is so large that it is incomprehensible, yet God created it.

- Our Father put the stars in their place and calls them by name.

- There is nothing God cannot do and nothing He does not know.

- The God who knows the limits of the Universe knows our limits too.

- This majestic God, who created the Universe, is with us.

Beautiful World

Genesis 1:20 (MSG)

God spoke:
Swarm, Ocean, with **fish** and all sea life!
Birds, fly through the sky over Earth!

Wow! I wish I could swim through the ocean!

The oceans are full of amazing creatures – and God made them all!

Have you ever seen a goldfish in a tank? Perhaps you have one in your house, or you've seen some at a pet shop. They're just one kind of fish – but there are thousands and thousands more. The rivers and oceans are bursting with them. And they all came from God's amazing imagination!

The Bible says that God filled the oceans with all kinds of sea creatures – wobbly jellyfish, clever octopuses, graceful dolphins, mighty whales and many more! And that's not all He made. The Bible says that He filled the sky with birds of all shapes, sizes and colours – from little sparrows in the back garden to bright parrots in the rainforests. He made them all, and He loves them all. **Isn't God amazing?**

TALK TOGETHER

How many kinds of fish can you find around you? You could visit an aquarium, or even just your local pet shop or garden centre. What about birds? See how many different kinds of birds you can spot in your garden or local park. You could look at pictures of fish and birds online or in books. Which species do you like the best?

MAKE TOGETHER

God made all kinds of fish and birds. Make a bird feeder/fat ball for the birds. See instructions on **page 46.**

PRAY TOGETHER

WOW, GOD! Thank you for weird and wonderful fish in the sea. Thank you for bright birds with beautiful voices. Thank you for everything that You've made! **Amen.**

Beautiful World

TIME TO REFLECT

Genesis 1:20-23 *(read more in Matthew 6:25-33)*

And God said, "Let the water teem with living creatures, and let birds fly above the earth across the vault of the sky." So God created the great creatures of the sea and every living thing with which the water teems and that moves about in it, according to their kinds, and every winged bird according to its kind. And God saw that it was good. God blessed them and said, "Be fruitful and increase in number and fill the water in the seas, and let the birds increase on the earth." And there was evening, and there was morning – the fifth day.

The Universe declares God's majesty; the oceans declare His might. We see God's benevolence in the trees and flowers. Living creatures – fish, birds and animals – are equally wonderful: a credit to the amazing Creator who made them. But seen through the lens of Scripture, they also provide a case study in God's love for us. Take birds, for example. Jerusalem in Jesus' day was overrun with sparrows. These small, common birds were generally considered of very little value – a pair sold for a penny to the poor for use in the temple. Yet, when Jesus is trying to teach his disciples how much they matter to God, it's the sparrows he turns to. Small as they are, God cares for them. He has His eye on them. And, He says, you're worth so much more than they are (Matthew 10:29-31).

These words echo those in the Sermon on the Mount in Matthew 6:26. Consider the birds of the air, Jesus says. They don't worry about where their next meal is coming from – God feeds them. And the conclusion Jesus draws on both occasions is the same.

IF GOD CARES FOR THE BIRDS, HOW MUCH MORE WILL HE CARE FOR YOU?

It's a message that speaks right to the heart of us. Even on a good day, as we're floored by the wonder of creation, we can feel small and insignificant. And on a bad day, when we feel like life is just too much to cope with, we can feel alone and downright forgotten. But the birds remind us that we are neither. God knows each one of us. He knows our situation. He knows our needs. And we are more precious to Him than we can dare to dream.

TIME TO ACT

1 Jesus tells us that we don't need to worry about our material needs – food, clothes, etc. – because God provides. Claim God's promise. Ask Him now for anything that you need.

2 Take some time to pray for the needs of people in your family, community or even nation. Could you be the answer to their prayers?

TIME TO PRAY

God of the sparrows,
I praise You that nothing is too small for Your notice, and no one too small for Your care.

Thank you that You care for me more than I could ever imagine.

Amen.

ONLY GOT A MINUTE?

- Living creatures – fish, birds and animals – are all made by God.

- Jesus said, "If God cares for the birds, how much more will He care for you?"

- When we feel small and insignificant, the birds remind us we are neither.

- God knows each one of us.

- We are more precious to Him than we can dare to dream.

Beautiful World

God made all kinds of amazing animals

Genesis 1:24-25 (MSG)

God spoke... and there it was: wild animals... cattle... every sort of reptile and bug.

Wow! Imagine having a nose like an elephant, or a big, long neck like a giraffe!

The world is full of amazing animals. God has a BIG imagination!

How many animals do you know? Think about farm animals – can you name ten? What about jungle animals – can you name another ten? What about pets? The world is FULL of incredible animals, reptiles and insects. And God made all of them!

The Bible says that God filled the world with animals – big ones, small ones, fluffy ones and fierce ones. Cows, sheep, cats and dogs. Huge elephants, tiny mice, tall giraffes, wriggly caterpillars and many, many more! There are literally MILLIONS of different kinds of animals and insects on our planet – and that includes some we've not even discovered yet. But even though *we* don't know them all, God knows them and loves them. **Isn't God amazing?**

TALK TOGETHER

How many different animals can you find this week? You could visit a farm, or the zoo, or even just a pet shop. You could look up different animals from around the world online or in a book. Ask an adult to read out some facts about the different animals you find. Which are your favourites? Why? Are there any particular animals you'd like to see?

MAKE TOGETHER

God made the animals and the insects. Make a paper-chain caterpillar. Add some antennae using pipe cleaners or cardboard and stick on googly eyes. Or make insects out of kitchen rolls/pipe cleaners/googly eyes, etc.

PRAY TOGETHER

WOW, GOD! Thank you for amazing animals and creepy crawlies. Thank you for things that run and things that wriggle. Thank you for everything You've made! **Amen.**

Beautiful World

TIME TO REFLECT

Genesis 1:24-25 (*read more in John 10:1-10*)

And God said, "Let the land produce living creatures according to their kinds: the livestock, the creatures that move along the ground, and the wild animals, each according to its kind." And it was so. God made the wild animals according to their kinds, the livestock according to their kinds, and all the creatures that move along the ground according to their kinds. And God saw that it was good.

Of all the animals on our planet, one finds itself mentioned in the Bible more than any other: the humble sheep. And no wonder. This farmyard favourite has been a staple of civilisation for thousands of years. Many of the heroes of the Old Testament kept sheep: Jacob, Moses and David to name but three. Jesus himself spoke about sheep – most famously in Luke 15 and John 10. The ins and outs of shepherding would've been familiar to people in Biblical times. The shepherd collected his sheep in the morning. He'd lead them out to the green pastures nearby. He watched over them as they fed, protecting them from predators and finding any that wandered off. It provided the perfect image to describe God's relationship with His people, found throughout the Old Testament. *"The Lord's my Shepherd, I'll not want,"* sang David (Psalm 23:1), overwhelmed by God's committed care. *"We all, like sheep, have gone astray,"* said Isaiah (Isaiah 53:6), explaining humankind's tendency to wander and God's willingness to rescue.

But what's striking when Jesus talks about Himself as the Good Shepherd is not just His care. It's His intimacy. Contrary to popular opinion, sheep do not aimlessly follow the crowd.

IN BIBLICAL TIMES, THERE WAS A STRONG BOND BETWEEN A SHEPHERD AND HIS SHEEP. SHEPHERDS GAVE THEIR SHEEP NAMES, WHICH THEY KNEW.

And the sheep recognised their shepherd's voice, following when he – and only he – called. It's a picture of belonging – of being known and loved, and of knowing and loving in turn. We don't just worship a deity or serve a master. We don't just receive things from a bounteous benefactor. We belong to the One who calls us by name. And His love will never let us go.

TIME TO ACT

1   The prophet Isaiah writes:

He tends his flock like a shepherd: he gathers the lambs in his arms and carries them close to his heart; he gently leads those that have young.

Isaiah 40:11

During this busy season of life, as we carry our own young in our arms, think about what it means to be loved and carried by God.

2   In the Bible, Jesus is described as both the Lion of Judah and the Lamb of God. Write down what each of those pictures means to you. How does each one shape or challenge your idea of Jesus? What does it mean to follow one who is both a lion and a lamb?

TIME TO PRAY

O God my Shepherd,
I praise You because You know me
and call me by my name.

Thank you that I belong to You.

Help me to hear Your voice each day
and stay close to You in turn.

Amen.

BIG

ONLY GOT A MINUTE?

- God says we belong to Him, like sheep belonging to a shepherd.

- The shepherd names and knows his sheep.

- The sheep hear his voice and trust him.

- We belong to the One who calls us by our own name.

- His love will never let us go.

Beautiful World

God saw **all** that He had made, and it was **very good.**

Genesis 1:31

Love God, love the planet
LEARNING TO LOOK AFTER GOD'S CREATION AS A FAMILY

"The earth is the Lord's, and everything in it." Psalm 24:1

God made a beautiful world – one that He loves completely. And He gave us the responsibility to look after it for Him (Genesis 1:28). Part of loving God, then, is learning to care for His wonderful creation. We're never too young to begin! Here are some easy ways to love God's lovely world:

- **Love your animals.** Encourage your children to be involved with looking after any family pets. Make a bird feeder **(page 46)** or a bug hotel for some of the creatures that visit your neighbourhood. Why not consider sponsoring an endangered animal?

- **Walk more.** Not only does walking help reduce harmful carbon emissions, it also encourages you to see the wonder in the world around you. Leave the car at home for short journeys. If walking for fun, why not litter pick at the same time?

- **Compost your vegetable waste.** Build a compost bin in the garden. This cuts down on waste going into the household bin, while enriching your soil in turn. Talk about your compost bin's favourite food: vegetable peelings, egg shells, tea bags... And make sure everyone takes a turn to feed it.

- **Shop second-hand.** This saves on waste, saves you money and may benefit a good cause. And, of course, it's always great to donate! Is there anything you could give away instead of throw away?

- **Use less energy.** As a family, get used to switching lights/the TV/toys off when they're not in use. Do the laundry at a lower temperature. (Maybe even do less laundry!) If you haven't done so already, and if it's possible, why not switch to a renewable energy supplier too?

- **Reduce what you get.** Try to avoid getting single-purpose items which can only go in the bin. Take your own bags to the shops. Make a weekly meal plan. Only buy food that you need and use up any leftovers.

- **Reuse what you have.** Before buying anything new – even stuff you 'need' – ask yourself if you have something else that would do the job. Old ice-cream tubs that will do for storage, clothes you forgot you had... You'll be amazed what you find you already have when you stop and think about it!

- **Recycle what you use.** Lots of household waste is now easily recycled. Why not teach children how to recycle by turning it into a game? Keep different boxes for plastics, cardboard, paper and aluminium. Time trial the children to see who can sort the recycling out the most quickly!

- **Buy ethically.** Pick up items that are fair trade, ethical, recycled or recyclable whenever possible. As a family, learn the different signs on the packaging and talk about what they mean. See if you can spot the signs at the supermarket.

John 3:16 (MSG)

This is how much God loved the world: He gave his Son...

Wow! God made light, trees, fish, stars... and everything!

Yes, Hal. He made and loves it all. And there's something else He loves too – YOU!

The Bible says that God made this beautiful world and everything in it. But there was something really, really special that He had planned. Something that was even more amazing and even more wonderful than all the rest. **Us!**

God made us. And He loves us more than we can ever imagine. The Bible says that He loves us so much that He made Himself into a tiny human. He was born as a baby called Jesus. He came to live with us so that we could know Him better. And when He died, He made a special way for us to be friends with Him forever! God's love for us is bigger than the huge Universe He created. **Isn't God amazing?**

TALK TOGETHER

Talk about the people who are special to you. What do you love about them? Think about how you are special to God – and how much He loves you!

MAKE TOGETHER

God made us. He knows us – and He really, really loves us! Make some peg dolls. Using traditional wooden clothes pegs, draw a face and draw or add hair with wool. You can use pen to draw their clothes or use scraps of fabric to make skirts and tops. You can use pipe cleaners to make hands. As you do so, think how God made you, and how much He loves you!

PRAY TOGETHER

WOW, GOD! Thank you that You know me. Thank you that You love me. Thank you that, even though You are really, really BIG, You made Yourself into a teeny-tiny person so that I could be Your friend forever. **Amen.**

DEVOTION 7 GREAT IS OUR GOD

Beautiful World

LITTLE

TIME TO REFLECT

Genesis 1:26-28 *(read more in John 15:9-17)*

Then God said, "Let us make mankind in our image, in our likeness, so that they may rule over the fish in the sea and the birds in the sky, over the livestock and all the wild animals, and over all the creatures that move along the ground."

So God created mankind in his own image, in the image of God he created them; male and female he created them.

God blessed them and said to them, "Be fruitful and increase in number; fill the earth and subdue it. Rule over the fish in the sea and the birds in the sky and over every living creature that moves on the ground."

God reveals something of Himself through all He's made. This includes His last creation. On the sixth day, Genesis tells us, God created people, and He made them *"in His image"*. God modelled us on Himself. Put another way – at the dawn of creation, God invested something of His divine character in us. It's true that sin has marred our humanity and we've fallen from God's ideal for us. But His likeness is still there. The very best parts of humanity are those which echo something of God our maker – such as goodness, truth or creativity. And without a doubt, it's love – freely and sacrificially given – that declares Him the loudest.

The Bible says that when we are in Christ, we are a new creation (2 Corinthians 5:17).

GOD IS UNDERTAKING A HUGE RESTORATION PROJECT IN US, SO THAT HIS IMAGE IS SEEN MORE CLEARLY.

And the greatest work is love. Love is central to God's character. Throughout Scripture, love is shown to be our primary calling as His people. *"Love God"* and *"love your neighbour as yourself"* sum up the law and the prophets. Love is the last lesson Jesus teaches His disciples – in what He commands them at the Last Supper in John 15, and in what He shows them in His wonderful, remarkable sacrifice on the cross. Two thousand years ago, the invisible God made Himself plain for all to see in Jesus. Today, He wants to do the same again – this time, through us. And it's as we learn to receive God's love and give it wholeheartedly to others that the awesome, loving God of creation truly becomes visible.

TIME TO ACT

1   Take some time to reflect on these words from Genesis 1:27:

God created humankind in His own image.

Let the words *'in His own image'* wash over you. What does it mean to you to be made in God's image? Write down some words or draw a picture in response.

2   It's not just 'me' who is made in God's image. Every one of us is made by God – precious to Him and bearing His likeness. How does this impact the way you see your neighbours? Your colleagues? The people in your community? How can you help them to see God through your loving words and actions?

TIME TO PRAY

O God, my God –
I praise You because You've known me and loved me from the very beginning.

I give myself to You now. Help me to live in the light of Your love.

Make me into what You always planned for me to be – for Your glory.

Amen.

ONLY GOT A MINUTE?

- God created us and made us *"in His image"*.

- Every one of us is made by God and we are precious to Him.

- We model the likeness of Christ.

- As we become more like God, as we receive His love and give it wholeheartedly to others, the awesome, loving God of creation truly becomes visible.

Beautiful World

Romans 1:20 (LWC)

I look at Your world. It shows me You're **awesome** and **loving.**

WOW! The world is AMAZING!

It is, Hal. But there's something even more amazing than this world. The awesome God who made it!

Our world is amazing. There's so much to make you say WOW! Big, blue skies. Giant, green trees. Bright, colourful flowers. Enormous elephants and tiny ants. Whales and dolphins, eagles and penguins – and so much more. And that's just on Earth! Look up into the sky at night and you'll see a million stars shining bright.

The Bible says that God made this wonderful world. It is His amazing artwork. Mountains, oceans, stars, fish, birds and animals – they all came from His BIG imagination. And He knows and cares for everything He made – including us. So next time you see something that makes you say WOW, turn it into worship. What a beautiful world. **And what an AWESOME God!**

TALK TOGETHER

Talk about all you've learnt about God's beautiful world together. What are your favourite animals, birds or fish? Why do you like them so much? Are there any places you love to visit – like the seaside or the woods? What do you love about them?

MAKE TOGETHER

God has made a beautiful world! Make some 'creation' biscuits. Cut them out using different shapes from creation – animal shapes, stars, flowers or people! As you bake, thank God for everything He has made.

LITTLE

PRAY TOGETHER

WOW, GOD! You are AMAZING! Thank you for the beautiful world that You made. Thank you that You love and care for everything in it – including me. I love You, God! **Amen.**

Beautiful World

TIME TO REFLECT

Romans 1:20

For since the creation of the world God's invisible qualities – his eternal power and divine nature – have been clearly seen, being understood from what has been made, so that people are without excuse.

Our world is incredible. And it points us towards God. The Bible says that there's something about exploring creation that helps us to grasp God Himself. It shows us God's 'eternal power'. Certainly, when we look at the mountains and the oceans, we get a sense of the limitless might of the God who made them. When we gaze up into the starry skies, we're overwhelmed by the size and the majesty of the God who put them in their place. And creation shows us God's 'divine nature'. Whether it's the delicate ecosystems – plants and living creatures working together and depending on each other to sustain life – or simply the irrepressible vegetation that returns year on year, nature testifies to a generous, caring God who fills the world with good things and provides for all He has made.

CREATION ITSELF IS A MIRACLE. AND THE MORE WE DISCOVER, THE MORE WONDERFUL IT SEEMS.

But this naturally begs the question: how often do we open ourselves up to experience its wonder? Every now and again we might be struck by the sight of a sunset, or by the star-speckled Universe surrounding us. But the rest of the time we're often too busy or distracted or disconnected to

really appreciate the amazing world around us. There's a strong case, however, for making wonder in creation part of our lives – ultimately because it helps us to see the God it reveals and leads us to worship Him. And so, as we journey through this beautiful world, may we learn each day to see more of the might, the majesty, the benevolence and – above all – the incredible love of its awesome Creator.

TIME TO ACT

1 As you go through the day, make a conscious decision to find wonder in God's world. See all that God has given you – for example, the natural world around you, the food you have to eat, etc. Remember to say thank you!

2 Look over the list of ways to find wonder as a family on **page 23**. Select one that you could do this week to help build 'wonder worship' into your family life.

TIME TO PRAY

God of creation,
I praise You for the extraordinary
and beautiful world You have made.

How great You are, Lord.

Amen.

ONLY GOT A MINUTE?

- Our world is incredible. It points us towards God, showing us God's 'eternal power' and His limitless might.

- The more we discover, the more wonderful we realise God is.

- How often do we open ourselves up to experience the wonder of creation around us?

- Pause and make space to stop and wonder.

- How can you bring 'wonder worship' into your family life?

BIG

Beautiful World

Crafts and recipes

DEVOTION 5   BIRD FEEDER/FAT BALL

For a bird feeder:

- Pipe cleaner
- Cereal hoops
- Ribbon

1   Thread cereal hoops onto a pipe cleaner.

2   Mould the pipe cleaner into a circle shape and tie together.

3   Finish with a ribbon and hang up for the birds to enjoy.

For a fat ball pine cone:

- Pine cone
- Ribbon
- Seed-based bird food
- Peanut butter or lard

1   Tie a ribbon around the top of the pine cone so you can hang it on a branch.

2   Squish peanut butter or lard into the pine cone using your hands.

3   Roll the pine cone in bird seed.

4   Make sure it is really full so that the birds have lots of yummy food!

5   Hang up in your garden or a local park.

DEVOTION 1

DEVOTION 2

DEVOTION 3

Blow painting: light pictures

Mountain range collage

3D daffodils

DEVOTION 8   CREATION BISCUITS

You will need:

- 100g (4oz) Cheddar or other hard cheese, grated
- 400g (16oz) plain flour
- ½ tsp baking powder
- Salt and freshly ground black pepper, to taste
- 100g (4oz) butter, softened

1   Preheat oven to 200°C/180°C fan/gas mark 6 and grease a baking sheet or line with greaseproof paper.
2   Combine grated cheese, flour, baking powder, salt and pepper in a bowl.
3   Mix in butter and lightly knead into a dough either by hand or with an electric mixer.
4   Roll the dough out with a rolling pin so it is about 1cm thick.
5   Cut biscuits out into different animal and creation shapes and put on the baking sheet.
6   Put in the oven to cook for 10-12 minutes until golden.

DEVOTION 4

Cardboard star mobile

DEVOTION 6

Caterpillar paper chain

DEVOTION 7

Peg dolls

Beautiful World

thank you prayers

Thank you, God, for Your whole world.

Thank you for windy rivers.

Thank you for tall mountains.

Thank you for green trees.

Thank you for blue seas.

Thank you for beautiful flowers.

Thank you for all the creatures.

Thank you for starry nights.

Thank you for my family... and me!

Thank you, God, that You have
the whole world in Your hands.

Amen.

Also available from Little WORSHIP Company

The **Little Worship Company** offers a range of inspiring products, including DVDs, an app **(Little Worship Company World)**, devotionals, curriculums and books. Our products are filled with beautifully-produced worship videos, prayers, games, stories and Bible quotes.

Each DVD follows a devotional journey, teaching your child timeless Bible truths. The DVDs and app have been created to help adults and children to discover God together at home, at church or out in the community.

 info@littleworshipcompany.com　 Littleworshipcompany　 @littleworshipcompany

Little Worship Company World

Worship anytime, anywhere

Through our digital world, hosted by the entertaining **Looyah family,** you and your child will be taken on a journey through beautifully-produced worship videos, games, stories, Bible quotes and age-appropriate studies. Each week there will be a new exciting journey of content to explore, as you and your little one discover God together.

 Download on the App Store　 GET IT ON Google Play　 Available at amazon